Becky Goldsmith & Linda Jenkins

COVERED with LOVE

Kids' Quilts & More
from **Piece O' Cake Designs**

C&T PUBLISHING

Text and Artwork © 2006 Becky Goldsmith and Linda Jenkins

Artwork © 2006 C&T Publishing, Inc.

Publisher: Amy Marson

Editorial Director: Gailen Runge

Acquisitions Editor: Jan Grigsby

Editor: Lynn Koolish

Technical Editors: Teresa Stroin and Deborah Dubois

Copyeditor/Proofreader: Wordfirm Inc.

Cover Designer: Kristy Zacharias

Page Layout Artist: Kerry Graham

Illustrators: Becky Goldsmith and Kirstie L. Pettersen

Production Assistant: Zinnia Heinzmann

Photography: Luke Mulks unless otherwise noted

Published by C&T Publishing, Inc., P.O. Box 1456, Lafayette, CA 94549

Library of Congress Cataloging-in-Publication Data

Goldsmith, Becky

Covered with love : kids' quilts & more from Piece O' Cake designs / Becky Goldsmith and Linda Jenkins.

p. cm.

Includes index.

ISBN-13: 978-1-57120-354-0 (paper trade : alk. paper)

ISBN-10: 1-57120-354-0 (paper trade : alk. paper)

1. Machine appliqué--Patterns. 2. Machine quilting--Patterns. 3. Children's quilts. I. Jenkins, Linda, 1943- II. Piece O'Cake Designs. III. Title. IV. Title: Kids' quilts and more from Piece O' Cake Designs.

TT779.G62945 2006

746.46'041--dc22

2006011189

Printed in China

10 9 8 7 6 5 4 3 2 1

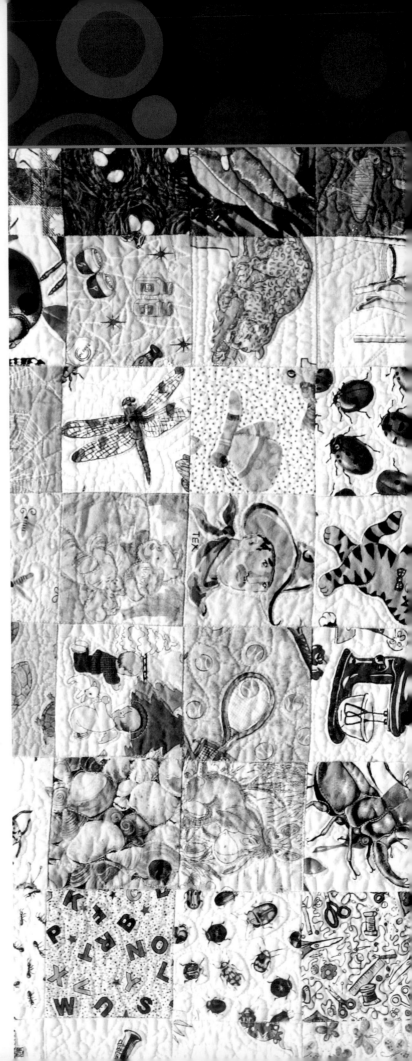

CONTENTS

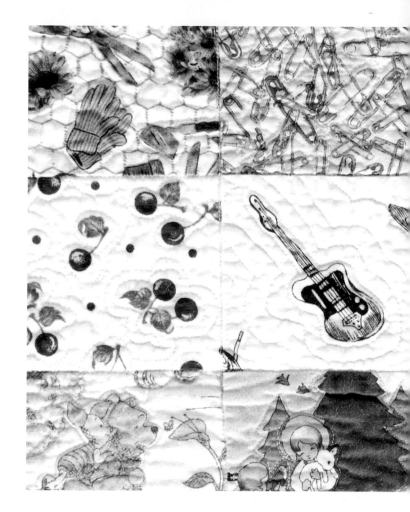

Acknowledgments

We've said it before and we'll say it again—we are very lucky to be associated with C&T! Everyone there has been very good to us. First, Todd Hensley, CEO, welcomed us with open arms. Amy Marson, Publisher, is always there to support us. Lynn Koolish, our editor, helps us make each book the best it can be. We thank them all.

It would be nice to be perfect but we aren't, so we are very grateful to Teresa Stroin, our technical editor, who makes sure that we get the details right. Luke Mulks, our photographer, makes everything look beautiful. Zinnia Heinzmann, the production assistant, keeps everything in order. Kerry Graham, this book's page layout artist, has given *Covered with Love* its cheerful and happy appearance. Kristy Zacharias designed a fabulous cover. We thank you all for your excellent efforts.

Dedication

Elanor

From Becky...

I'm a grandmother! I love my sons, but what they say is true—grandchildren are just wonderful! Elanor is three years old as I write this. She is at our house often and it's fun to experience what little kids are like again.

Elanor has been my inspiration for this book. I realized when she was born how important it was for me, a quilter, to make quilts for her. They truly do cover her with my love—like a hug from Nana.

From Linda...

When I think of children and quilts, I think of my husband's Grandma Vestal. She made hand-quilted quilts for her children and grandchildren. Lots and lots of quilts. We have always had her quilts to sleep under and to use to add warmth to our decor. She made beautiful quilts and utility quilts. She gave us love in so many ways, but her quilts live on long after she has left us and truly cover us in her love.

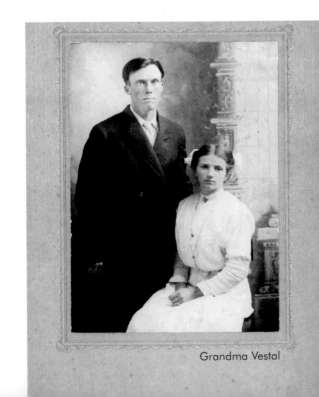

Grandma Vestal

Introduction

Children are everywhere but you don't really notice them much unless they are yours. We both raised two sons. While they were growing up they were a major part of our daily lives. And then our children grew up and we moved on to life without kids in the house. Neither one of us has been particularly interested in making children's quilts—until now!

When we began thinking about designing the quilts for this book we realized that children of different ages require different kinds of quilts. We decided that, while we love little bitty babies, we would have more fun designing for the toddler to eight-year-old age range.

Children love to explore their environment. Toddlers see the same things we do but they have no idea what they are looking at. Every day is full of new things to learn about. I Spy quilts are fascinating to small children. Becky's granddaughter, Elanor, has spent countless hours exploring the designs on the many fabrics in her I Spy quilt.

The *Animal Parade* bed quilt combines counting, the alphabet, and cute animals that children love.

It's a great quilt for a child's first big bed. Linda used colors that are suitable for either boys or girls, but this is an easy quilt to color to go with the decor in any child's room.

Have you seen the card-table tents on pages 36–39 yet? Becky's mom, Elizabeth Eckroat, made tents like this for Becky and her brother and sister when they were little. Elizabeth made one for Elanor (her great-granddaughter) too and we decided that they had to be included in this book. These tents are easy to make and kids love them. Consider painting a floor-cloth to go with your tent. We'll show you how!

Scrapbooking has become very popular in the last few years. While we will always be quilters first, we admit that scrapbooking can be fun. C&T has developed blank board books for scrapbookers (imagine a kid's board book with nothing in it). We think they are perfect for making storybooks tailored to a specific child. Children love stories about people and things in their very own lives. Write your own stories or use ours to make a book for the special child in your life.

We really enjoyed working on the projects in this book. It was fun to think like a child again. We hope you enjoy making them as much as we did!

Casual appliqué is a machine appliqué technique that we came up with for the projects in this book that we didn't want to hand appliqué. Some quilts are made to be used; of course hand appliqué will withstand daily use, but we didn't want to spend the time that hand appliqué takes on quilts that will be subjected to hard use and lots of washing.

Neither of us is a fan of fusible web. It is stiff and we don't like our appliqué to be stiff. In addition we don't trust the chemicals in fusible web or fabric glues. It is our opinion that only time will tell how they affect the fabric and that time will come too late for us. So we didn't fuse the appliqué pieces to the quilt—we pinned them in place, then we used free-motion stitching and matching thread on the sewing machine to sew the appliqué pieces to the quilt blocks. In some cases we added a blanket stitch or free-motion zigzag on the outer edges of the appliqué.

If you have done free-motion quilting before, this is going to be very easy for you. If you have not done free-motion quilting, this is a great place to practice. Once your quilt is layered and basted, your quilting stitches will work with the free-motion stitches to firmly hold the appliqué in place.

This is a raw-edge appliqué technique. The amount of stitching you do near the edges of the appliqué will determine the amount of fraying. We think this technique is especially suited to children's quilts that have large pieces and/or busy fabric. Read more about it on pages 57–58.

We used both hand and casual appliqué for the projects in this book. Use whichever technique you prefer.

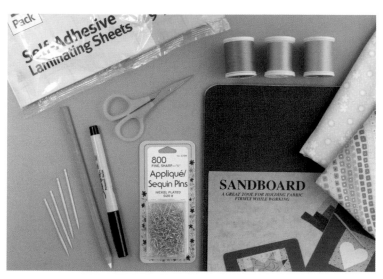

Appliqué supplies

Supplies

Fabric: All the fabrics used in these quilts are 100% cotton. *Always prewash your cotton fabric.* This is especially important for the casual appliqué technique.

Appliqué thread: Use cotton thread with cotton fabric. There are many brands to choose from. Work with different brands until you find the ones that work best for you. For hand appliqué, we can recommend DMC 50-weight machine embroidery thread, Aurifil 50-weight cotton thread, Mettler 60-weight machine embroidery thread, and YLI's Soft Touch cotton thread. All are two-ply threads.

Machine quilting thread: Use cotton thread with cotton fabric. We most often use the thread listed above for our machine quilting. We like a lot of quilting in our quilts so this works well. If you plan to quilt far apart you should use a heavier thread.

Hand quilting thread: Use cotton thread with cotton fabric. We like Gütermann's hand quilting thread.

Pins: In needle-turn hand appliqué, use ½″ sequin pins to pin the appliqué pieces in place.

In casual appliqué, use long, fine, glass-head pins.

Use larger flower-head quilting pins to hold the positioning overlay in place where necessary.

Needles: For hand appliqué, we use a size 11 Hemming & Son milliner's needle. There are many good needles. Find the one that fits *your* hand.

Scissors: Use embroidery-size scissors for both paper and fabric. Small, sharp scissors are better for intricate cutting.

Rotary cutter, mat, and acrylic ruler: When trimming blocks to size and cutting borders, rotary cutting tools will give you the best results.

Pencils: We use either a General's Charcoal White pencil or an Ultimate Mechanical Pencil for Quilters to draw around templates onto the fabric.

Permanent markers: To make the positioning overlay (refer to page 51), a black Sharpie Ultra Fine Point Permanent Marker works best on the upholstery vinyl.

Quilter's Vinyl: Use 18″-wide Quilter's Vinyl to make the positioning overlay (see Resources on page 63). If you can't find Quilter's Vinyl, you can also use clear, medium-weight upholstery vinyl from a store that carries upholstery fabric. Keep the tissue paper that comes with it.

Clear, heavyweight self-laminating sheets: Use these sheets to make templates. You can find them at most office supply stores, online, (see Resources) and sometimes at warehouse markets. Buy the single-sided sheets, not the pouches. If you can't find the laminate, use clear Contac paper—it'll work in a pinch.

Sandpaper board: Our favorite sandpaper board has fine-grain sandpaper glued to a sheet of Masonite. When tracing templates onto fabric, place the fabric on the sandpaper side of the board. Then place the template on the fabric. You'll love the way the sandpaper holds the fabric in place when you trace.

Wooden toothpick: Use a round toothpick to help turn under the turn-under allowance at points and curves. Wood has a texture that grabs and holds the fabric.

Fusible web: If you prefer to fuse and machine stitch the appliqué, use a paper-backed fusible web. Choose the one you like best and follow the directions on the package. It's a good idea to test the fusible web on the fabric you will be using.

Non-stick pressing sheet: If you are doing fusible appliqué, a non-stick pressing sheet will protect the iron and ironing board.

Full-spectrum work light: These lamps give off a bright and natural light. A floor lamp is particularly nice as you can position it over your shoulder. Appliqué is so much easier when you can see what you are doing.

> **Note:** We use Ott lights and love them. But be aware that they are full-spectrum lights containing UV rays. We keep our lights positioned so that they shine onto our appliqué but not into our eyes.

Batting: We prefer to use a cotton batt. Some of our favorites are Hobbs Organic Cotton and Dream Cotton Select.

Quilting gloves: Gloves make it easier to hold onto the quilt during machine quilting. We like the Machingers brand.

Sewing machine: Successful machine quilting requires the best sewing machine and table that you can afford. We love our Berninas! The new Bernina 440 with the stitch regulator is particularly suited for free-motion quilting.

Fabric Preparation

Prewash your fabric before using it. Prewashing is a good way to test for colorfastness and shrinkage. Different fabrics shrink at different rates. It's better if the fabric bleeds or shrinks *before* it is sewn into the quilt. Prewashed fabric has a better hand and it smells better. But the best reason to prewash is that it makes the fabric easier to appliqué.

It is very important to prewash your fabric if you plan to use the casual appliqué technique. The appliqué pieces will stick to each other better, making it much easier to sew, and the raw edges of the appliqué will fray less.

About Our Fabric Requirements

Cotton fabric is usually 40″ to 44″ wide off the bolt. To be safe, we calculated all our fabric requirements based on a 40″ width.

Use the fabric requirements for each quilt as a guide, but remember that the yardage amounts will vary depending on how many fabrics you use and the sizes of the pieces you cut. Our measurements allow for both fabric shrinkage and a few errors in cutting.

Audition Your Fabric

We cut and place every fabric in position on the wall before we take a stitch. Always! By doing this we *know* that the quilt is going to be wonderful *before* putting all those stitches into it.

First put your backgrounds up on the design wall. If you are going to piece your backgrounds, put all the pieces on the wall. Only sew the background blocks together when you are sure they are balanced and work well together.

Start with block 1. Trace and cut out the appliqué pieces. Start with whatever piece seems like the most obvious choice to you. If you are hand appliquéing add the ³⁄₁₆″ turn-under allowance and cut carefully. Use your overlay and place each piece on the wall as you go.

Each fabric is auditioning for its role in the quilt. Some fabrics are going to get the hook. Others will be perfect. You really don't know until you see them in place on the wall. *You can't fake the audition.* Sticking some fat quarters up on the wall and hoping for the best doesn't work. We know.

You will find out, as you read further, that some appliqué shapes are easier to sew if you cut them out leaving excess fabric around them. This is especially true of small, narrow, or pointy shapes. That means that you won't get to use every appliqué piece that you have on the wall. Some will be sacrificed. But your quilts will be so much better if you audition every fabric.

When the fabrics in block 1 are perfect, move on to block 2. Continue until all the appliqué pieces are on the wall, even the borders. Place sashing strips and inner borders—everything that is part of that quilt—on the wall. Are you done?

Take a giant step back and really look at your quilt. Squint at it, use a reducing glass, take a picture—do whatever you need to do to help you evaluate your quilt. You are done when you are happy.

Seam Allowances

All machine piecing uses ¼″ seam allowances except the card-table tents, which use ½″ seam allowances.

Borders

The cutting instructions in this book are mathematically correct. However, variations in the finished size of the quilt top can result from slight differences in seam allowances. You should always measure *your* quilt before adding the borders. When measuring, be sure to measure the inside of the quilt top, not the outer edges, which can stretch. Adjust the size of your borders if necessary.

Hand Appliqué or Fusible Web?

We prefer not to use fusible web in our appliqué—you may like it. Luckily we can each have it our own way. If you choose to use fusible web, please test the fabrics you plan to use. We recommend that you stitch around the outside of all fused appliqué pieces either by hand or machine. Use a matching thread if you want your stitching to be less visible.

Pick-Up STICKS

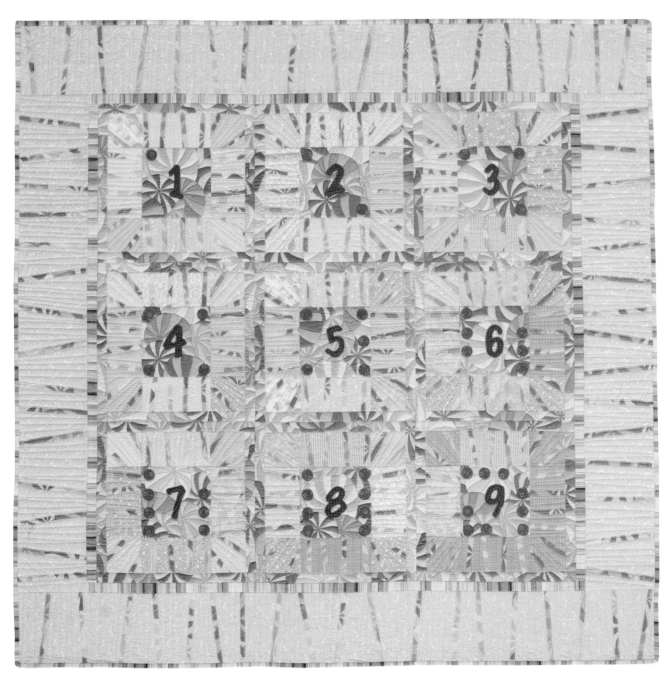

Made by Becky Goldsmith, 2005
Finished quilt size: 64″ × 64″

Do you remember playing pick-up sticks when you were little? It was simple but fun—just like this quilt. Becky made her quilt in softer colors, but this pattern would be just as cute in brights.

Materials

Multicolored print for block backgrounds, sashing, and appliquéd strips: 2½ yards

A variety of yellow fabrics for the block and outer border backgrounds: 4⅝ yards

Note: If you do not want to piece your outer border, you need 2 continuous yards of outer border fabric. If you do not want to piece your inner border, you need 1½ continuous yards of inner border fabric.

Striped inner border fabric: ⅜ yard

Orange appliqué fabric: ¼ yard

Binding: 1 yard

Backing and sleeve: 4⅛ yards

Batting: 70″ × 70″

Cutting

Multicolored print

Block center backgrounds:

A: Cut 9 squares 9½″ × 9½″.

Appliquéd strips:

Cut 216 strips ½″ × 6½″ *on the bias* to be used in the blocks.

Cut 68 strips ½″ × 10″ *on the bias* to be used in the borders.

Block sashing:

D: Cut 18 strips 1½″ × 14½″.

E: Cut 18 strips 1½″ × 16½″.

Yellow fabrics

Block border backgrounds:

B: Cut 36 strips 6″ × 9½″.

C: Cut 36 squares 6″ × 6″.

Outer border backgrounds:

F: Top and bottom outer borders: Cut 3 strips 9½″ × 40″; construct 2 strips 9½″ × 52½″.

G: Side outer borders: Cut 4 strips 9½″ × 40″; construct 2 strips 9½″ × 66½″.

Striped fabric

Top and bottom inner borders: Cut 3 strips 1½″ × 40″; construct 2 strips 1½″ × 48½″.

Side inner borders: Cut 3 strips 1½″ × 40″; construct 2 strips 1½″ × 50½″.

Orange fabric

Cut the numbers and circles for casual appliqué as directed below.

Binding

Becky used a striped fabric that would have looked funny on the diagonal (bias), so she cut 8 strips 2½″ × the width of the fabric on the straight of grain and sewed them together end to end. Under most circumstances we recommend bias binding. Cut 1 square 27″ × 27″ to make a 2½″-wide continuous bias strip approximately 273″ long. (Refer to pages 54–55 for instructions.)

Cut fabric for appliqué as needed.

Block Assembly

Refer to pages 47–53 for instructions on making the positioning overlay and preparing the appliqué. Appliqué patterns are on the pullout at the back of the book. Refer to pages 57–58 for casual appliqué instructions.

1. Make templates for numbers 1–9 and for circle 1.

2. Draw a 7″ × 7″ square on a piece of paper. Draw horizontal and vertical centerlines in the square. Place the template for the number 1 in the center of the square and trace around it. Refer to the photo and place the template for circle 1 in the square and trace around it as well. This is your pattern for the center of block 1. Repeat for blocks 2–9. Make your placement overlays from these patterns.

3. Place the blocks, sashing, and inner and outer borders on the design wall. Place the appliqué pieces on the wall. Play with the placement of all pieces until you are happy with the way your quilt looks.

4. Appliqué each block A center using the casual appliqué technique. When your appliqué is complete, press the blocks on the wrong side. Trim each block to 7½″ × 7½″.

5. Place 4 strips ½″ × 6½″ on a block B background as shown. Pin them in place. Appliqué the B blocks using the casual appliqué technique. When your appliqué is complete, press the blocks on the wrong side. Trim each block to 4″ × 7½″.

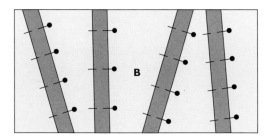
Appliqué B blocks.

APPLIQUÉING THE STRIPS

It is very important to cut these ½″-wide strips on the bias of the fabric. If you cut them on the straight of grain the raw edges will ravel too much.

Becky found that it was easier to sew these strips to the backgrounds with a regular straight stitch (not a free-motion stitch). She used a straight-stitch foot with the feed dogs up. The straight edges of the strips were easier to manage this way.

6. Place and then pin 2 strips ½″ × 6½″ on a block C background. Appliqué the C blocks using the casual appliqué technique. When your appliqué is complete, press the blocks on the wrong side. Trim each block to 4″ × 4″.

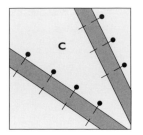
Appliqué C blocks.

7. Sew the blocks together. Press the seams in alternate directions. Add the D and E block sashing. Press toward the sashing.

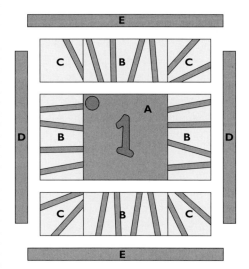
Sew blocks together.

8. Place and then pin 15 strips ½″ × 10″ on each outer border F background and 19 strips ½″ × 10″ on each outer border G background. Refer to the Quilt Assembly Diagram for strip placement. Appliqué the borders using the casual appliqué technique. When your appliqué is complete, press the borders on the wrong side. Trim each border F to 7½″ × 50½″ and each border G to 7½″ × 64½″.

Quilt Assembly

Refer to the Quilt Assembly Diagram for quilt construction.

1. Sew the sashed blocks into rows. Press the seams in alternate directions.

2. Sew the rows together. Press toward the bottom.

3. Sew the top and bottom inner borders to the quilt. Press toward the inner border.

4. Sew the side inner borders to the quilt. Press toward the inner border.

5. Sew the top and bottom outer borders (F) to the quilt. Press toward the inner border.

6. Sew the side outer borders (G) to the quilt. Press toward the inner border.

7. Layer and baste the quilt. Quilt by hand or machine. (Refer to page 54.)

8. Bind the quilt. Add a label and sleeve if desired. (Refer to pages 55–56.)

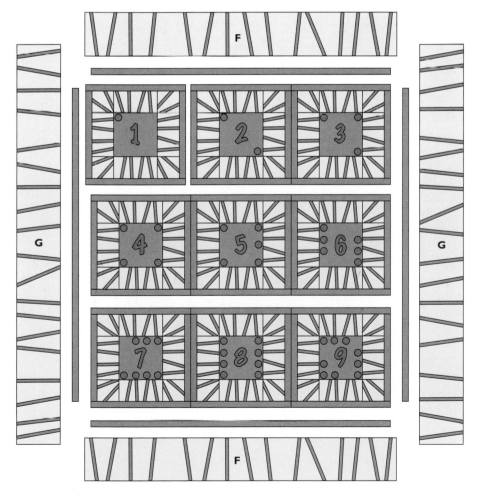

Quilt Assembly Diagram

Made by Linda Jenkins, 2005
Finished quilt size: 38″ × 48″

*Linda's daughter-in-law, Viviana, has a sister who was having a baby as we were working on this book. Viviana asked Linda if she **might** be able to make a quilt that had a jungle theme. What perfect timing. So Linda made this quilt especially for Viviana's nephew, Matthew.*

Materials

This is a scrappy quilt. Use the yardage amounts below as a guide. They will vary with the number of fabrics you use.

Green background: A variety to total 1½ yards

Appliqué fabrics: A variety of large scraps

Orange inner border fabric: ⅓ yard

Green border fabric: ⅝ yard

Binding: ¾ yard

Backing and sleeve: 2⅔ yards

Batting: 44″ × 54″

Special Supplies for the Eyes

White acrylic paint: Linda used Liquitex brand Professional Acrylic Artist Color—Heavy Body.

Black permanent gel pen

Stencil brush with fine, pointed tip

White charcoal pencil

Special supplies for eyes

Cutting

Green background fabric

Background pieces:

  A: Cut 2 squares 10½″ × 10½″.

  B: Cut 4 squares 12″ × 12″.

  C: Cut 6 rectangles 10½″ × 12″.

Orange fabric

Side inner borders: Cut 2 strips 1½″ × 40½″.

Top and bottom inner borders: Cut 2 strips 1½″ × 32½″.

Green border fabric

Side outer borders: Cut 3 strips 3½″ × 40″; construct 2 strips 3½″ × 42½″.

Top and bottom outer borders: Cut 2 strips 3½″ × 38½″.

Binding

Cut 1 square 22″ × 22″ to make a 2½″-wide contin-uous bias strip approximately 184″ long. (Refer to pages 54–55 for instructions.)

Cut fabric for appliqué as needed.

Block Assembly

Refer to pages 47–53 for instructions on making the positioning overlay and preparing the appliqué. Appliqué patterns are on page 18 and on the pullout at the back of the book.

1. Sew the green background pieces together. Press the seams in alternate directions. There is a center horizontal seam that you can use to place your positioning overlay. Press to create a vertical centerline. Refer to the assembly diagrams on pages 16 and 17.

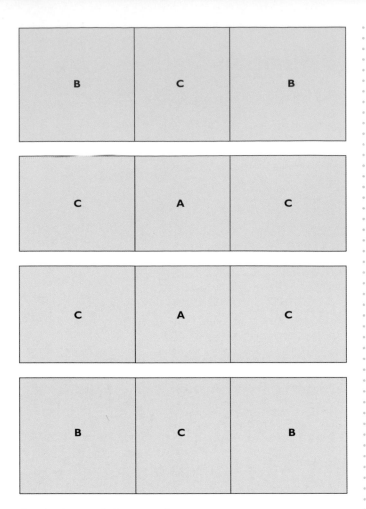

Sew background pieces together.

2. Linda used a lion, snake, giraffe, hippo, monkey, turtle, and zebra. Use different animals if you prefer. Use the smaller-sized animal patterns that are on the pullout. They fit this quilt better. Make a copy of each animal you choose. If you use 2 of any animal, make 2 copies of it.

3. Make 6 copies of the Grass 1 pattern and make 8 copies of the Grass 2 pattern.

4. Draw a 30˝ × 40˝ rectangle on a piece of paper. Tape pieces of paper together as necessary. Draw horizontal and vertical centerlines in the rectangle. Follow the Quilt Assembly Diagram and place the copies of the animals on the paper. Tape the animals in place. Position the grass in the same manner. For the grass, trace only the part that is inside the 30˝ × 40˝ rectangle. This is your pattern. Make your 30˝ × 40˝ placement overlay from this pattern.

5. Cut out your animal appliqué pieces. Then refer to pages 32–33, Steps 3–7, and paint the faces on the animals.

6. Appliqué the quilt. There are 4 tufts of grass that extend over the borders. Appliqué them after you attach the borders. When your appliqué is complete, press the quilt on the wrong side. Trim it to 30½˝ × 40½˝.

Quilt Assembly

Refer to the Quilt Assembly Diagram for quilt construction.

1. Sew the side inner borders to the quilt. Press the seams toward the inner border.

2. Sew the top and bottom inner borders to the quilt. Press the seams toward the inner border.

3. Sew the side outer borders to the quilt. Press the seams toward the border.

4. Sew the top and bottom outer borders to the quilt. Press the seams toward the border.

5. Appliqué the remaining tufts of grass. Press on the wrong side.

6. Layer and baste the quilt. Quilt by hand or machine. (Refer to page 54.)

7. Bind the quilt. Add a label and sleeve if desired. (Refer to pages 55–56.)

Quilt Assembly Diagram

CRITTERS
Grass Templates

Grass 1

1

2

Grass 2

Made by Becky Goldsmith, 2005
Finished quilt size: 29″ × 35″

If asked to draw a picture of his or her house, a young child might very well draw a picture that looks like this quilt. Bright and cheerful, it's perfect to hang in a child's room.

Materials

This is a scrappy quilt. Use the yardage amounts below as a guide. They will vary with the number of fabrics you use.

Yellow house block background: ⅝ yard

Graduated yellow-to-green house block background: ⅝ yard

Chartreuse flower block backgrounds: ⅓ yard

Green fence and signature block backgrounds: ½ yard

Appliqué fabrics: A variety of large scraps

Binding: ⅔ yard

Backing and sleeve: 2 yards

Batting: 32″ × 41″

Embroidery floss for hair, sun face, dog face and chimney smoke

Cutting

Yellow fabric

House block 1 background: Cut 1 rectangle 17½″ × 26½″.

Graduated yellow-to-green fabric

House block 2 background: Cut 1 rectangle 26½″ × 17½″.

Becky used a yellow background for house block 1 and appliquéd grass. For house block 2, she used a graduated yellow-to-green fabric. If you choose to use the same yellow background for both blocks, appliqué grass onto block 2.

Chartreuse fabric

Flower block backgrounds: Cut 2 rectangles 7½″ × 17½″.

Green fabric

Fence block backgrounds: Cut 3 rectangles 10½″ × 7½″.

Signature block background: Cut 1 square 7½″ × 7½″.

Binding

Becky used a striped fabric that would have looked funny on the diagonal, so she cut 5 strips 2½″ × the width of the fabric on the straight of grain and sewed them together end to end. Under most circumstances we recommend bias binding. Cut 1 square 20″ × 20″ to make a 2½″-wide continuous bias strip approximately 149″ long. (Refer to pages 54–55 for instructions.)

Cut fabric for appliqué as needed.

Block Assembly

Refer to pages 47–53 for instructions on making the positioning overlay and preparing the appliqué. Appliqué patterns are on page 22 and on the pullout at the back of the book.

1. Make templates and overlays for My House block 1, My House block 2, and the Fence block.

2. Make 4 copies of Flower A, 2 copies of Flower B, and 2 copies of Flower C from My House block 2.

APPLIQUÉ TIPS

Use *cutaway appliqué* for the small and narrow pieces such as flower stems, shoes, and so on; *circle appliqué* on the flower centers, wheels, and heads; *off-the-block appliqué* for the sun and doors, and *reverse appliqué (off-the-block)* on the windows. Refer to pages 59–61 for instructions.

3. Draw a 5″ × 15″ rectangle on paper. Refer to the Quilt Assembly Diagram and place the flower copies inside the drawn rectangle and tape them down. Draw horizontal and vertical centerlines in the rectangle. This is your pattern for Flower block 3. Repeat for Flower block 4. Make your placement overlays from these patterns.

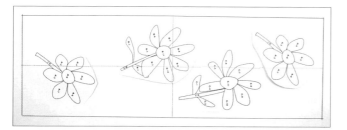

Tape copies to paper pattern.

4. Appliqué My House blocks 1 and 2. Embroider the hair on the family, the faces on the sun and the dog, and the smoke from the chimney. When your blocks are complete, press them on the wrong side. Trim each block to 24½″ × 15½″.

5. Appliqué Flower blocks 3 and 4. When your appliqué is complete, press the blocks on the wrong side. Trim each block to 5½″ × 15½″.

6. Appliqué 3 Fence blocks. When your appliqué is complete, press the blocks on the wrong side. Trim each block to 5½″ × 8½″.

7. Appliqué or embroider the signature block. When your appliqué is complete, press the block on the wrong side. Trim the block to 5½″ × 5½″.

SIGNATURE BLOCK

The 5″ × 5″ block in the lower right-hand corner of the quilt is the perfect place to personalize this quilt. Appliqué or embroider your name, the date, whom you made the quilt for—anything that is pertinent to your quilt.

Quilt Assembly

Refer to the Quilt Assembly Diagram for quilt construction.

1. Sew the blocks together into rows. Press the seams in alternate directions.

2. Sew the rows together to form the body of the quilt. Press the seams in the easiest direction.

3. Layer and baste the quilt. Quilt by hand or machine. (Refer to page 54.)

4. Bind the quilt. Add a label and sleeve if desired. (Refer to pages 55–56.)

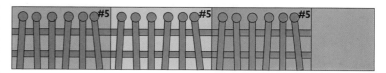

Quilt Assembly Diagram

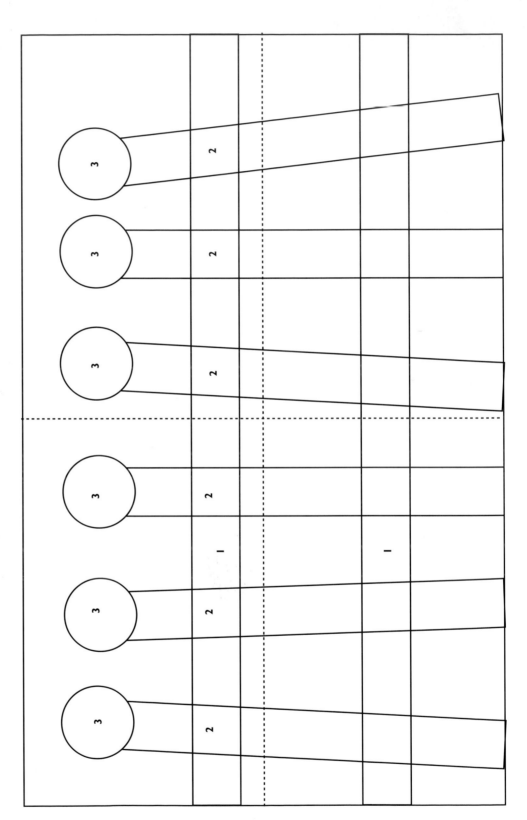

Fence block pattern

Made by Becky Goldsmith, 2005
Finished quilt size: 50″ × 50″

You can't really appreciate an I Spy quilt until you have seen a child with one. Becky's granddaughter, Elanor, absolutely loves hers! She is all over it (and it is all over her) as she discovers and rediscovers the hidden pictures.

WHAT IS AN "I Spy" QUILT?

We used conversation prints in both of the I Spy quilts in this book. A conversation print is a fabric that has pictures of things on it. It can be just about anything—bugs, bicycles, clouds, dogs, teapots, and so on—the list is endless. Once you start collecting these prints it's hard to stop.

Conversation prints are pretty busy. They are so busy that a quilt made from them can be hard for a grown-up to look at for very long! But a child tends to look at small areas of a quilt—not the quilt as a whole. To a child, these busy, interesting fabrics offer endless hours of fun!

Materials

This is a scrappy quilt made from many conversation prints. Group your prints into light and medium to dark stacks. You will want lots of small pieces of conversation prints. Becky's quilt has about 75 different fabrics in it. Use the yardage amounts below as a guide. The amount of fabric you use will vary with the number of different fabrics in your quilt.

Becky chose to arrange the border blocks in her quilt by color. She clustered the darker hearts at the center of the quilt.

Light conversation prints:
A variety to total 2¼ yards

Medium to dark conversation prints:
A variety to total 1⅞ yards

Binding: ⅞ yard

Backing and sleeve: 3⅜ yards

Batting: 56″ × 56″

Cutting

Light fabrics

Block backgrounds: Cut 16 squares 12½″ × 12½″.

Border squares: Cut 10 squares 5½″ × 5½″.

Medium to dark fabrics

Border squares: Cut 26 squares 5½″ × 5½″.

Hearts: Cut 64 hearts (pattern on page 26) for casual appliqué.

Leaves: Cut 64 leaves (pattern on page 26) for casual appliqué.

Binding

Cut 1 square 24″ × 24″ to make a 2½″-wide contin-uous bias strip approximately 217″ long. (Refer to pages 54–55 for instructions.)

Block Assembly

Refer to pages 47–53 for instructions on making the positioning overlay and preparing the appliqué. Appliqué patterns are on page 26. Refer to pages 57–58 for casual appliqué instructions.

1. Place the background blocks on your design wall. Place the hearts and leaves on each block. Play with their placement until you are happy with the way your quilt looks.

2. Place the border blocks around the quilt, again playing with their placement until you are happy with the way your quilt looks.

3. Make your templates and overlay. (Note that the pattern on page 26 is half of the block.)

4. Appliqué each block. This a good quilt to make using the casual appliqué technique.

5. When your appliqué is complete, press each block on the wrong side.

6. Trim the blocks to 10½″ × 10½″.

Quilt Assembly

Refer to the Quilt Assembly Diagram for quilt construction.

1. Sew the blocks into rows. Press the seams in alternate directions.

2. Sew the rows together. Press toward the bottom.

3. Sew the side border squares into rows. Press toward the top.

4. Sew the side borders to the quilt. Press toward the border.

5. Sew the top and bottom border squares into rows. Press in alternate directions.

6. Sew the top and bottom borders to the quilt. Press toward the border.

7. Layer and baste the quilt. Quilt by hand or machine. (Refer to page 54.)

8. Bind the quilt. Add a label and sleeve if desired. (Refer to pages 55–56.)

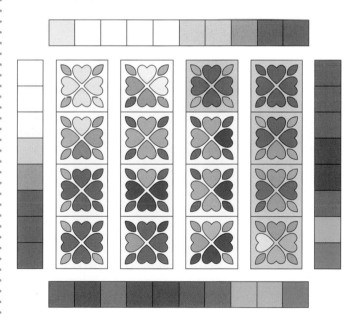

Quilt Assembly Diagram

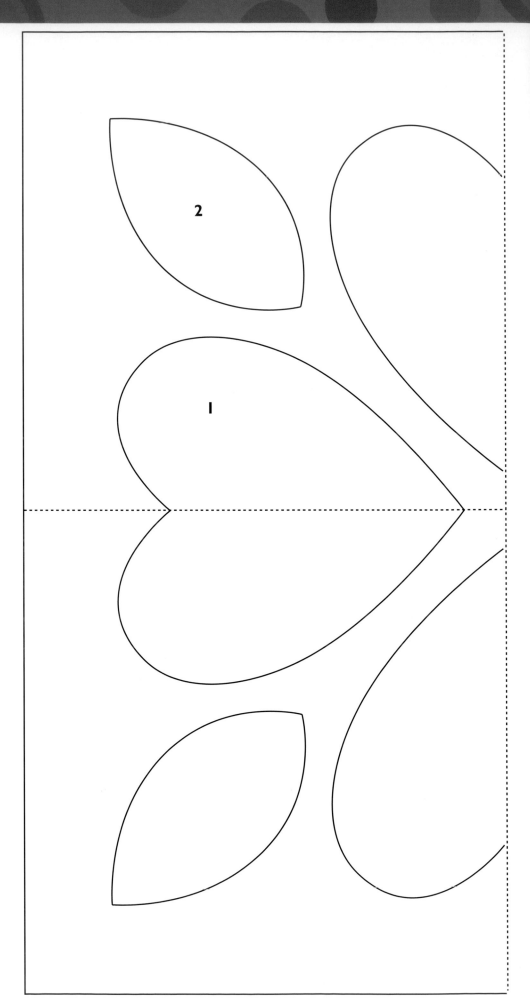

Covered with Love

Trace this half Heart block twice on your overlay vinyl to complete the pattern.

Made by Becky Goldsmith, 2005
Finished quilt size: 48″ × 48″

Fun and fast to make—this is a great I Spy quilt that kids love!

Materials

This is a scrappy quilt made from many conversation prints. Group your prints into light and medium-dark stacks. You will want lots of small pieces of conversation prints. Becky's quilt has over 100 different fabrics in it. Use the yardage amounts below as a guide. The amount of fabric you use will vary with the number of different fabrics in your quilt.

Becky chose to arrange the squares in her quilt by value. She clustered the lightest squares in the center and the darkest squares at the outside of the quilt.

Light conversation prints: A variety to total 1 yard

Dark conversation prints: A variety to total 1½ yards

Binding: ⅞ yard

Backing and sleeve: 3¼ yards

Batting: 54″ × 54″

Cutting

Light fabrics

Cut 100 squares 3½″ × 3½″.

Dark fabrics

Cut 156 squares 3½″ × 3½″.

CUTTING BIGGER BLOCKS

Some conversation-print designs are bigger than 3″ × 3″. Feel free to cut bigger squares or rectangles to best show off the design in the fabric. Look closely and you'll see that Becky did just that. Be sure that the shape you cut has a finished size that is divisible by 3. Remember to add a ¼″ seam allowance to each side.

Binding

Cut 1 square 23″ × 23″ to make a 2½″-wide continuous bias strip approximately 207″ long. (Refer to pages 54–55 for instructions.)

Quilt Assembly

Refer to the Quilt Assembly Diagram for quilt construction.

1. Place your squares on your design wall. Here comes the fun part! Play with the placement of the squares until their arrangement makes you happy.

2. Sew the blocks into rows. Press the seams in alternate directions.

3. Sew the rows together. Press toward the bottom.

4. Layer and baste the quilt. Quilt by hand or machine. (Refer to page 54.)

5. Bind the quilt. Add a label and sleeve if desired. (Refer to pages 55–56.)

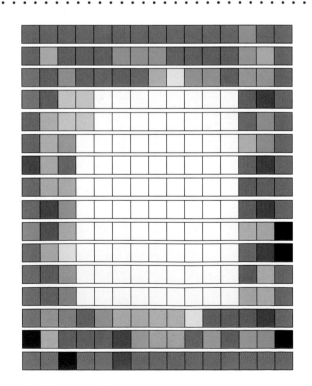

Quilt Assembly Diagram

Animal PARADE

Made by Linda Jenkins, 2005
Finished quilt size: 72″ × 90″

What child wouldn't want this as a bed quilt? There's so much to look at. Count the circles inside the stars, learn the alphabet, and name the animals. This is a great quilt for both boys and girls.

Materials

This is a scrappy quilt. Use the yardage amounts below as a guide. They will vary with the number of fabrics you use.

Yellow block and border backgrounds: A variety to total 5 yards

Blue stars: A variety to total 2⅝ yards

Red and orange print inner border: ⅝ yard

Appliqué fabrics: A variety of large scraps

Binding: 1 yard

Backing and sleeve: 5⅞ yards

Batting: 78″ × 96″

Special Supplies for the Eyes

White acrylic paint: Linda used Liquitex brand Professional Acrylic Artist Color—Heavy Body.

Black permanent gel pen

Stencil brush with fine, pointed tip

White charcoal pencil

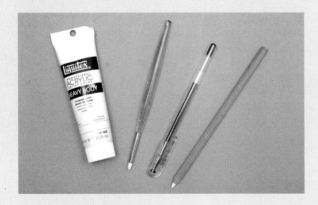

Special supplies for eyes

Cutting

Yellow fabrics

Star block backgrounds: Cut 18 strips 4″ × 40″; cut 60 squares 4″ × 4″ and 60 rectangles 4″ × 7½″.

Side border backgrounds: Cut a variety of strips 16½″ wide; construct 2 strips 16½″ × 78½″.

Bottom border background: Cut a variety of strips 16½″ wide; construct 1 strip 16½″ × 74½″.

Blue fabric

Block centers: Cut 4 strips 9½″ × 40″; cut 15 squares 9½″ × 9½″.

Star points: Cut 12 strips 4″ × 40″; cut 120 squares 4″ × 4″.

Red and orange print fabric

Top and bottom inner borders: Cut 3 strips 3½″ × 40″; construct 2 strips 3½″ × 42½″.

Side inner borders: Cut 4 strips 1½″ × 40″; construct 2 strips 1½″ × 76½″.

Binding

Cut 1 square 30″ × 30″ to make a 2½″-wide continuous bias strip approximately 341″ long. (Refer to pages 54–55 for instructions.)

Cut fabric for appliqué as needed.

Block Assembly

Refer to pages 47–53 for instructions on making the positioning overlay and preparing the appliqué. Appliqué patterns are on the pullout at the back of the book.

1. Make templates for numbers 1–15 and for circles 1 and 2.

2. Draw a 7″ × 7″ square on a piece of paper. Draw horizontal and vertical centerlines in the square. Place the template for the number 1 in the center of the square and trace around it. Refer to the photo and place the template for the Star block circle 1 in the square and trace around it as well. This is your pattern for the center of block 1. Repeat for each block. Note that blocks 13, 14, and 15 use smaller numbers and also use the template for circle 2. (Refer to the Quilt Assembly Diagram on page 33.) Make your placement overlays from these patterns.

APPLIQUÉ TIPS

Use *cutaway appliqué* for the narrow pieces such as the legs, trunks, tails, and snake. Refer to page 59 for instructions. You can also use *casual appliqué*, refer to pages 57–58 for instructions.

3. Appliqué the block centers. When your appliqué is complete, press the blocks on the wrong side. Trim each block to 7½″ × 7½″.

4. Draw a diagonal line on the wrong side of each blue 4″ × 4″ square. Place a square on a 4″ × 7½″ yellow rectangle as shown. Sew on the diagonal line.

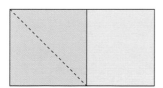

Sew on the diagonal line.

5. Cut away the excess fabric, leaving a ¼″ seam allowance.

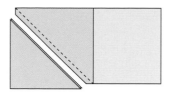

Cut away excess fabric.

6. Press the seams toward the blue triangle.

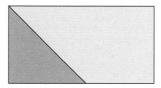

Press.

7. Place a square on the other side of the rectangle as shown. Sew on the diagonal line.

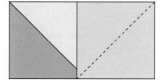

Sew on the diagonal line.

8. Cut away the excess fabric, leaving a ¼″ seam allowance.

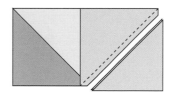

Cut away excess fabric.

9. Press the seams toward the blue triangle.

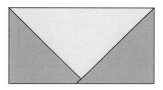

Press.

10. Place the appliquéd block centers with the rest of the block pieces on your design wall. Sew the pieces of the block together into 3 rows. Press the seams toward the blue triangles.

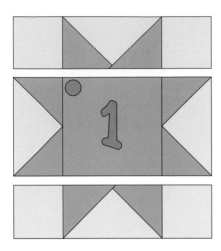

Sew pieces of block together into rows.

11. Sew the 3 rows together in each block. Press the seams in alternate directions.

Border Assembly

Refer to pages 47–53 for instructions on making the positioning overlay and preparing the appliqué. Appliqué patterns are on the pullout at the back of the book. Use the larger animals for this quilt.

1. Draw a 14″ × 76″ rectangle on a piece of paper. Draw vertical and horizontal centerlines. Refer to the illustration and place the appropriate templates in the rectangle and trace around them. This is your pattern for the left border. Repeat for the right border. Make your placement overlays from these patterns.

Left border

Right border

2. Draw a 14″ × 72″ rectangle on a piece of paper. Draw vertical and horizontal centerlines. Refer to the illustration and place the appropriate templates in the rectangle and trace around them. This is your pattern for the bottom border. Make your placement overlays from these patterns.

Bottom border

3. Cut out your animal appliqué pieces, then paint the faces on the animals. Place your fabric right side up on your sandboard. Refer to the pattern for placement and draw the outside edge of the eye with a white charcoal pencil. The outline helps keep the paint inside the eye.

4. Paint the entire eye white using the stencil brush. Use a light touch. Let the paint dry completely and then go back and touch up any areas that need it. Let the white paint dry for several hours.

5. Draw the outline of the pupil on each eye with a black permanent gel pen. Fill it in with the gel pen.

6. Draw the noses and mouths with a black gel pen.

7. Let the faces dry for several hours. Iron them from the back of your block to heat set the paint.

ABOUT THE PAINT

There are a variety of artist-grade acrylic paints and gel pens on the market. Some will work better than others. Be sure to test the paint you buy for fastness before you paint the faces on your animals.

8. Appliqué the borders. When your appliqué is complete, press the borders on the wrong side. Complete the giraffe appliqué after the border is sewn to the quilt.

9. Trim the side borders to $14\frac{1}{2}'' \times 76\frac{1}{2}''$.

10. Trim the bottom border to $14\frac{1}{2}'' \times 72\frac{1}{2}''$.

HANDLING LONG OVERLAYS

Pin the overlay near the piece you are about to position. Roll up the excess overlay so that you can more easily handle it. Then position your appliqué pieces.

Quilt Assembly

Refer to the Quilt Assembly Diagram for quilt construction.

1. Sew the blocks together into rows. Press the seams in alternate directions.

2. Sew the rows together to form the body of the quilt. Press the seams in the easiest direction.

3. Sew the top and bottom inner borders to the quilt. Press the seams toward the inner border.

4. Sew the side inner borders to the quilt. Press the seams toward the inner border.

5. Sew the side borders to the quilt. Press the seams toward the inner border. Complete the giraffe appliqué.

6. Sew the bottom border to the quilt. Press the seams toward the inner border.

7. Layer and baste the quilt. Quilt by hand or machine. (Refer to page 54.)

8. Bind the quilt. Add a label and sleeve if desired. (Refer to pages 55–56.)

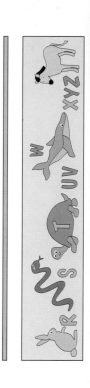

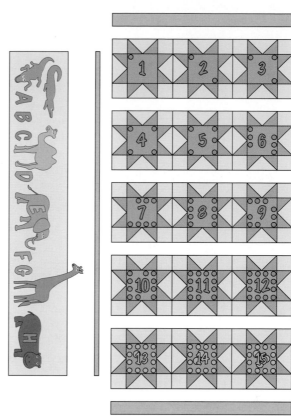

Quilt Assembly Diagram

PILLOWCASES

Made by Linda Jenkins, 2005
Finished size: 30″ × 20″
(fits standard pillow)

You've made a quilt for your favorite youngster; why not make a special pillowcase to go with it? In fact, why not make two? Use coordinating fabrics to make a very cheerful room.

Materials

Makes one standard-size pillowcase.

Main fabric: ⅞ yard

Contrast strip: ⅛ yard

Hem: ⅜ yard

Appliqué fabrics: a variety of large scraps

Cutting

Main fabric

Cut 1 piece 25½″ × 40½″.

Contrast strip fabric

Cut 1 strip 1½″ × 40½″.

Hem fabric

Cut 1 strip 9½″ × 40½″.

Cut fabric for appliqué as needed.

Pillowcase Assembly

1. Sew the main fabric, the contrast strip, and the hem together. Press the seams toward the hem.

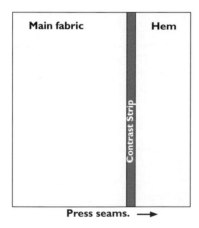

Sew together main fabric, contrast strip, and hem.

2. Topstitch the seams.

3. Press under ¼″ at the outer edge of the hem.

APPLIQUÉ TIPS

Use *cutaway appliqué* for the narrow pieces such as the legs, trunks, tails, and snake. Refer to page 59 for instructions. You can also use *casual appliqué*, refer to pages 57–58 for instructions.

4. Bring this pressed-under edge to the back so that it covers all the seam allowances on the wrong side of the pillowcase. Sew it in place with a straight stitch on your sewing machine.

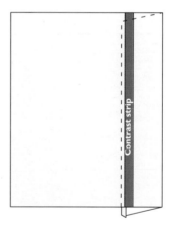

Bring hem to back, covering raw edges of seam allowances.

5. Appliqué the pillow. When the appliqué is complete, press the pillow on the wrong side.

6. Fold the pillowcase in half, right sides together, and sew the bottom and 1 long side together.

7. Finish the raw edges with an overlock or zigzag stitch.

8. Turn the pillowcase right side out and press.

9. Insert a pillow and enjoy!

Card-Table TENTS

Made by Elizabeth Eckroat, 2005
Fits a standard card table
34″ (w) × 34″ (d) × 28″ (h)

Becky remembers the tents her mom, Elizabeth Eckroat, made for her and her brother and sister. Inside the tent it was a different world— a place to play and dream and make believe! Becky's mom made tents for her grandsons and recently for her great-granddaughter, Elanor. Times may have changed but kids still love those card-table tents.

  Covered with Love

Materials

We designed our tents to fit a standard 34″ square by 28″ high card table, but please measure your card table before beginning. If your card table is a different size, adjust your cutting measurements accordingly. Add some extra tent and lining fabric (about 1 yard each) if your card table is bigger.

Tent fabric: 5¼ yards

Tent lining: 4¼ yards

Appliqué fabrics: A variety of large scraps

Fabric ties: ¼ yard

Ribbon ties (optional, instead of fabric ties): 4 yards

Binding: ¾ yard

Cutting

You may notice that we cut the tent top just a little bit small. Cotton does stretch some with use and we wanted to be assured of a snug fit.

Tent fabric

Tent top: Cut 1 square 34½″ × 34½″.

If your card table has rounded corners you can round the corners of the tent top. Be sure to match the curve in the card table when you cut. Rounded corners are a little easier to sew.

Tent sides: Cut 1 strip 148″ × 29″.

Lining fabric

Tent lining: Cut 1 strip 148″ × 29″.

Ties

Cut 4 strips 1½″ × 40″. Crosscut into 12 strips 1½″ × 12½″.

Binding

Cut 1 square 22″ × 22″ to make a 2½″-wide continuous bias strip approximately 180″ long. (Refer to pages 54–55 for instructions.)

Tent Assembly

Note: Use a ½″ seam allowance. Your tent will hold up better over time with a larger seam allowance.

1. Prewash your fabric. We believe that you should always prewash, but it's especially important here. Any tent that is used by a child is eventually going to need to be washed. Cotton fabric shrinks, so it makes sense to shrink it *before* you make your tent.

2. Place the tent side strip and the tent lining strip right sides together. Sew them together along 3 sides, leaving 1 long side open. **Remember to use a ½″ seam allowance.**

Place tent side and lining strips right sides together. Sew 3 sides.

3. Turn the long strip right side out. Press the edges. Topstitch ¼″ in from the sewn edges.

4. Place 3 marking pins 36¾″ apart along the long open side of the tent side strip.

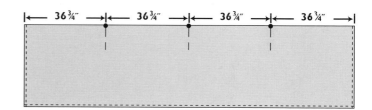

Place 3 pins 36¾″ apart.

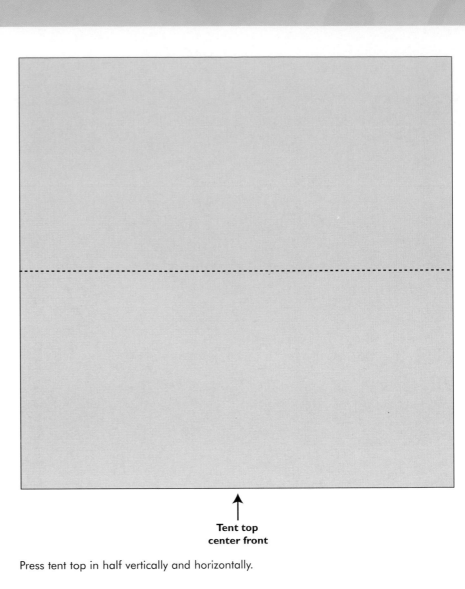

**Tent top
center front**

Press tent top in half vertically and horizontally.

5. Press the tent top in half vertically and horizontally. This creates a pressed-in center grid in the tent top.

6. Beginning at the center front and matching raw edges, place the lining side of the tent side strip against the wrong side of the tent top fabric. The exposed seams will be covered with bias binding.

7. Pin the tent side strip to the top, stopping 3″ away from the first corner you come to. Move farther down the length of the tent side strip to the first marking pin. Match this pin to the center of the next side of the tent top. Work back to the corner and pin the tent side strip to the tent top. Stop 3″ away from the corner.

8. There is extra fabric at the corners. Make a small pleat on either side of the corner to take up this fullness. Pin the pleats in place.

9. Continue working in this manner, pinning the tent side strip to the tent top. The far end of the tent side strip will butt up to the first end at the center front of the tent.

MAKING TIES

Cut 12 strips of fabric 1½″ × 12½″. Lightly press each strip in half lengthwise, right sides together. Sew down the length of each strip using a ¼″ seam allowance. Sew one end shut. Turn the strip inside out. Press. Topstitch to make the ties stronger.

10. Make 8 ties 12¼″ long (or use ribbon). Place the end of a tie into the pinned seam, 4″ away from a corner. The length of the tie should hang toward the lining. Repeat for the other side of the corner. Repeat for all corners. When the tent is in use, these ties are tied over the card-table legs, inside the tent, to hold it firmly in place.

Ties go around legs of card table, inside tent.

11. Sew the tent side strip to the tent top, as you have pinned it.

12. Bind the raw edges as you would the edges of a quilt. (Refer to pages 55–56 for bias binding instructions.) Match the raw edges of the folded binding with the raw edges of the exposed tent seam allowance. Sew together with a seam allowance slightly larger than ½″. This will ensure that the binding will cover the tent's seamline. Fold the binding over the raw edges and sew it down by hand or machine.

13. Make 4 ties 12¼″ long (or use ribbon). Sew one to each side of the tent opening so that the tent can be tied shut. It's also nice to be able to tie the tent open. Hold the tent flaps open to find the spot to attach the other 2 ties.

14. Embellish the tent as you wish. Add appliqué or embroidery! Remember to keep it safe—don't add embellishments that a child could choke on.

PAINT THE SKY

Becky painted the underside of her granddaughter Elanor's card table a rich twilight blue to look like the sky. You can add stars for a night sky or clouds for a daytime sky.

Polka-Dot FLOORCLOTH

Made by Becky Goldsmith, 2005
Finished floorcloth size: 45″ × 45″

It's really nice to have the perfect rug to put under the card-table tent—but the perfect rug is hard to find. It's a lot more satisfying to make your own. And it's really easy. Painted floorcloths have been around for hundreds of years. They are durable and inexpensive. Perfect for a child's play area.

Materials

Heavyweight canvas: Use a #10- or #12-weight canvas. We found ours online. A nice alternative is to use a heavy canvas dropcloth. Home improvement stores carry a variety of sizes.

Latex primer: Use tinted or white. It took every drop of a quart for our floorcloth. It makes sense to buy a gallon.

Short-nap roller brush, handle, and pan

Small bottles of acrylic paint (Ceramcoat or similar): These are available at craft stores; one bottle of each color should be sufficient.

1″ foam brushes

Duct tape

Water-based polyurethane: Use either the brush-on or spray-on variety.

Hot glue gun and hot glue sticks

Prepare the Canvas

1. Cut your canvas to 50″ × 50″.

2. Tape the canvas to a clean area of your garage floor or some other appropriate location.

3. Stir the primer and pour it in the paint pan. Use the roller to paint the canvas. Stop about 1″ from all the outside edges. Let the paint dry.

4. Remove the tape. Turn the canvas over and re-tape it to the floor. Paint the other side of the canvas with 2 coats of primer. Let it dry as directed between coats. This is the right side of the floorcloth.

5. When the canvas is completely dry, draw a 45″ × 45″ square on the right side of the floor-cloth with a pencil. Then draw a line 1½″ inside each side of the square to mark the border.

6. Refer to the Circle Placement Diagram and draw the circles on your floorcloth.

DRAWING THE CIRCLES

Becky used her dishes as templates for her circles. The largest, dinner-plate-sized circle is 10½″ in diameter. The salad plate is 8½″, the bread plate is 7⅜″, the bowl is 5½″, and the teacup is 3″.

Paint the Floorcloth

1. Choose the lightest value of paint that you will be using on your floorcloth. Shake that bottle of paint and then squirt a small amount onto a paper plate. Use a foam brush and begin painting.

2. Work from the center out. Paint each area that is the same color.

3. Wash and dry your brush. Get a new paper plate and paint the next darkest color. This paint dries pretty quickly so you shouldn't have to worry about smearing wet paint. Don't forget to paint the border.

4. When you have finished painting, let the floorcloth dry overnight. Spray or paint 2 coats of polyurethane over the right side of the floorcloth. Follow the directions and let the polyurethane dry completely.

5. Draw a line 1˝ away from the outer edge of the painted border. Draw a line on a 45° angle at each corner.

Draw line marking edge of hem. Draw angled line in each corner.

6. Cut away the excess canvas on the drawn line. Fold the hem to the back, creasing the fold.

7. Heat your glue gun. Turn the floorcloth upside down. Hot glue the hem to the backside of the floorcloth.

Hot glue hem to backside of floorcloth.

8. Some floorcloth painters advocate putting a coat of paste wax over the finished cloth to protect it. This can be renewed as needed

CARING FOR A FLOORCLOTH

- Place a waffle-weave rug pad underneath your floorcloth.

- Clean the floorcloth gently with a cloth and mild soapy water.

- Don't let your floorcloth get wet.

- When storing, roll it right side out; never fold it.

- Make sure the feet of your card table are covered with rubber tips or felt pads so they don't mar the surface of the floorcloth.

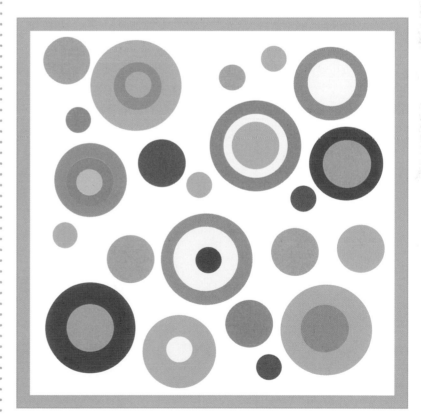

Circle Placement Diagram

Who's the baby?

Made by Becky Goldsmith, 2005

Children love books. They really love books that they can read themselves. Board books, with their sturdy cardboard pages, are perfect for small children. There are lots of cute board books in the stores, but you won't find one made especially for your favorite child.

Once you get started you'll find yourself coming up with all sorts of book ideas. Any person important in the life of the child can be included in your book. How about a book filled with special places—my house, my grandparents' house, my friend's house? Or a book of shoes? (Elanor loves shoes!) You don't really need to come up with a story—the images in the book tell the story. Elanor is very proud of herself when she reads her own special book. It makes her smile, and that's a wonderful thing to see!

Materials

We are quilters and of course we have lots of fabric! So we decided to cover our pages with fabric. Choose fabric that is colorful and that complements the photos.

We do not recommend adding any embellishments to the book that a child could pry off, put in his or her mouth, and choke on.

Fabric: Use a variety of small pieces to cover the pages.

Photographs: Select 14 photographs for book covers and pages.

Text: Print or write text for pages.

Blank board book: Use the size you prefer (see Resources).

Glue and protective finish: Use Mod Podge matte luster (the acid-free version is nice if you can find it) OR acrylic paint gel medium (usually near the acrylic tube paints); both are available at craft and art supply stores.

Small, sharp scissors: 4″ Omnigrid scissors worked best for us.

Brayer: This handy tool is like a rubber rolling pin with a handle; find it at a craft or art supply store.

1″ foam brushes

Paper towels

Waxed paper

Fine sandpaper: Use 210 or 220 grit.

Decorative papers (optional): We used fabric to cover our pages, but you can use paper if you prefer.

Special board book supplies

That said, we often find the background behind the people in a photo to be distracting. To help young readers focus on the people, trim away the background with short, sharp, precise scissors. It looks better if you leave just a tiny bit of background as an outline around the figure.

Trim photos leaving tiny outline around figures.

Preparing the Fabric

1. Press your fabric. Cut a piece of fabric ½″ bigger on 3 sides for each page, including the front and back covers. You'll trim the fabric to fit the page after everything is dry.

2. Plan which fabric will be on each page.

Preparing the Photos

Printing the Photos

Don't use your originals—make copies!

You will be painting Mod Podge over the photos. Some photos printed on home photo printers will smear. Becky made her copies on a Kodak photocopy machine. Test one photo with Mod Podge before making all your copies.

You can also use photos printed on plain paper from a color printer. The color may not be as intense, but plain-paper photos have a lower profile on the page and that can be nice. They glue down easily, but they can wrinkle if you use too much Mod Podge.

Cropping the Photos

A photo may be perfect just the way it is or you may want to crop it. You can also tear the edges, giving it a softer, more organic look.

Preparing the Text

You can hand write or use a computer for your text. Either way, choose a paper that looks good with your book. Adjust the length of your sentences to fit the available space. For handwriting, use a permanent pen.

You will be painting Mod Podge over the paper, so be sure to test both the paper and your written words before you prepare all the text.

Tear or cut text blocks apart.

Assembling the Book

Cover your work surface with paper or cardboard. Becky worked on an old rotary mat that she didn't care about. Place wax paper between the pages to prevent Mod Podge from seeping between the pages.

Covering the Pages

1. Apply Mod Podge to a page with a foam brush. The cardboard will soak it up just a bit, so keep brushing more on until the whole page is wet and tacky. Be sure to brush the Mod Podge all the way to the edges of the page, but don't overdo it. Wipe up any excess that flows over the sides of the page.

Apply Mod Podge to page.

2. Line up 1 edge of the fabric with the center crease of the book and carefully place the fabric on the page. If necessary, peel it up and reposition it—but add more Mod Podge so that the fabric sticks to the page. Make sure the entire page is covered.

Carefully place fabric on page.

3. Flatten the fabric onto the page with the brayer. The fabric may stretch as you roll it. Start out using gentle pressure; increase the pressure when you are sure the fabric is firmly in place.

Flatten fabric with brayer.

4. Glue fabric to the facing page. As the Mod Podge dries, move on to the rest of the pages. Keep waxed paper between the pages until you are sure they are dry. Finish by covering the front and back covers. Cover the spine with a separate strip of fabric.

5. After everything is dry, trim the fabric to the edges of the pages with a rotary cutter, scissors, or a fresh, sharp X-ACTO knife.

CARE OF FOAM BRUSHES

Wash out your foam brush if it's going to be more than a few minutes between coats. Squeeze the Mod Podge out of the brush and back into the bottle with your fingertips. Then wash the brush with water. Squeeze the excess water out of the brush with your fingers, then with a towel before using it again.

Adding the Photos and Text

1. Paint a layer of Mod Podge over the fabric on a page. Place the photo for that page into position. Be sure that you have enough Mod Podge behind it to hold it in place. Work out any air bubbles behind the photo with your fingertips.

Stick photo in place with Mod Podge.

2. Paint Mod Podge over the photo and beyond its edges. Feather this new Mod Podge onto the damp page. The foam brush will leave ridges on the photo. Do your best to smooth them out and keep them running either top to bottom or side to side. Keep the sides of the pages free from excess. The layer of Mod Podge over the photo acts as a sealer. It will dry clear.

Paint over photo.

3. As the Mod Podge dries you'll notice that the fabric starts to feel rough. When it is dry, lightly sand any rough areas. Avoid sanding the photos. If you notice that the sides of the pages are rough, sand them as well. Wipe away any dust. Keep your work surface clean.

Lightly sand rough areas.

Who's the daddy?

CURLING PAGES

You'll notice the pages curling just a bit as you work. They generally flatten out when both sides of the page are glued. Don't wait too long between gluing both sides of a page, as this will help keep the pages flat. Let the Mod Podge dry to the touch, then work on the back side of the page.

To flatten a book, let the book dry completely overnight—or longer. Then, place pieces of waxed paper between the pages and over the front and back covers. Place a heavy weight on the whole book. Leave it for 10 hours or more. This will flatten the pages pretty well. You may do this at any time during the making of the book as long as the pages are dry.

4. Place the paper with the text for a page right side down on waxed paper. Paint Mod Podge on the back of the paper. Stick it to the page. Paint a light coat of Mod Podge over the paper, being careful not to move, stretch, or wrinkle it. Repeat for all pages.

5. Paint a finish coat of Mod Podge on all pages. When the pages are dry, sand any rough areas and edges.

OTHER OPTIONS

If you don't want to cover your pages with fabric you can cover them with decorative papers. You can paint the pages with acrylic paint. You can use rubber stamps. The options are limitless!

Who's the mommy?

Elanor
is the baby.

General INSTRUCTIONS

We have a great way to do appliqué using sturdy laminated appliqué templates and a clear vinyl positioning overlay that makes it a snap to position all the pieces. If you are new to the appliqué techniques of Piece O' Cake Designs, read through this entire chapter before beginning a project.

For a more complete description of all our appliqué techniques, refer to our book The New Appliqué Sampler *and our DVD* Learn to Appliqué the Piece O' Cake Way!

Preparing the Backgrounds for Appliqué

Always cut the background fabric larger than the size it will be when it is pieced into the quilt. The outer edges of the block can stretch and fray as you handle it while stitching. The appliqué can shift during stitching and cause the block to shrink slightly. For these reasons it is best to add 1″ to all sides of the backgrounds when you cut them out. We have included this amount in the cutting instructions for each quilt. You will trim the blocks to size after the appliqué is complete.

1. Cut the backgrounds as directed in the project instructions. For blocks with pieced backgrounds, cut and sew them together as directed.

2. Press each background block in half vertically and horizontally. This establishes a center grid in the background that will line up with the center grid on the positioning overlay (refer to page 51).

3. Use a pencil to draw a ¼″-long mark at the end of each of the pressed-in grid lines. Be sure not to make the lines too long or they will show on the block. These little lines will make it easier to correctly position the overlay as you work with it and will help you find the center when trimming your block.

4. Use a pencil to draw a little X in *one corner* of the block background. This X will be in the same corner as an X that you will draw on the overlay. Be sure to mark the X near the edge so it won't show on the finished block.

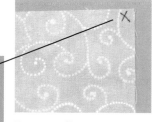

Draw small X in one corner.

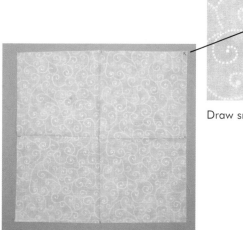

Draw ¼″-long lines at each end of pressed-in grid.

Press to create center grid.

Making the Appliqué Templates

Each appliqué shape requires a template, and we have a unique way to make templates that is both easy and accurate.

1. Use a photocopier to make 2–3 copies of each block or appliqué pattern. If the pattern needs to be enlarged or reduced, make these changes *before* making copies. Always compare the copies with the original to be sure they are accurate.

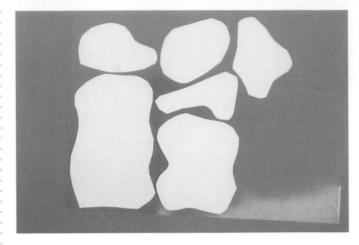

Place appliqué shapes *drawn* side down on self-laminating sheets for hand appliqué and casual appliqué.

DETERMINING THE NUMBER OF COPIES

You need a complete paper shape for each appliqué piece that requires a template. When one shape lays over another you need 2 copies. Look at each shape to determine how many copies it requires—or make 3 copies of each one knowing that you'll probably have some extra copies.

Place appliqué shapes *blank* side down on self-laminating sheets for fusible appliqué.

2. Cut out the appliqué shapes from these copies. Cut them in groups when you can—it saves on the laminate. Leave a little paper allowance around each shape or group. Where one shape overlaps another, cut the top shape from one copy and the bottom shape from another copy.

3. Place a self-laminating sheet shiny side down on the table. Peel off the paper backing, leaving the sticky side of the sheet facing up.

4. If you are doing **hand appliqué** or **casual appliqué**, place the templates *drawn* side down on the self-laminating sheet. For **fusible appliqué**, place the *blank* side down. Take care when placing each template onto the laminate. Use more laminating sheets as necessary.

We have reservations about recommending the use of fusible web. It is stiff and we aren't sure how the chemicals in it will affect the fabric over time. However, if you choose to use fusible web, follow the manufacturer's instructions. Use a non-stick pressing cloth to protect the iron and ironing board from the fusible web. Be sure to test the fabrics you plan to use. Iron the fusible web to the *wrong* side of the appliqué fabric. Do not peel off the paper backing until you are ready to use the appliqué.

Iron fusible web to wrong side of fabric.

5. Cut out each shape. Try to split the drawn line with your scissors—don't cut inside or outside the line. Keep edges smooth and points sharp.

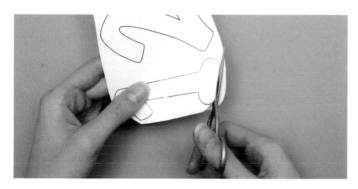

Cut out each template.

You'll notice how easy these templates are to cut out. That's the main reason we like this method. It is also true that a mechanical copy of the pattern is more accurate than hand tracing onto template plastic. As you use the templates, you will see that they are sturdy and hold up to repeated use.

MAKING BIG TEMPLATES

The animals are big—some are bigger than a sheet of paper. When this is the case, copy the shape onto as many sheets of paper as necessary. Overlap and tape the copies together to make the whole shape. Place the shape on laminate as described above. Overlap pieces of laminate as necessary to cover the whole shape.

Using the Templates

The templates for each block are numbered. The numbers indicate the stitching sequence. Begin with #1 and work your way through the block. The templates are used with the shiny laminate side up. **Hand appliqué** and **casual appliqué** templates are placed with the drawn, shiny side up on the right side of the fabric. **Fusible appliqué** templates are placed on the wrong side of the fabric with the blank, shiny side up.

1. For **hand appliqué** and **casual appliqué**, place the appliqué fabric right side up on a sandpaper board (refer to page 8). For **fusible appliqué**, place the fabric with the wrong side up. (The fusible web side will be up.)

2. Place the template right side up (shiny laminate side up) on the fabric with as many edges as possible on the diagonal grain of the fabric. A bias edge is easier to turn under (hand appliqué) and will fray less than one on the straight of grain.

3. Trace around the template. The sandpaper board will hold the fabric in place while you trace. Make a line you can see! Be sure to draw the line right up next to the edge of the template. It won't matter if the line is wide. It gets turned under in hand appliqué and cut off in casual appliqué and fusible appliqué.

Trace onto fabric for hand appliqué or casual appliqué.

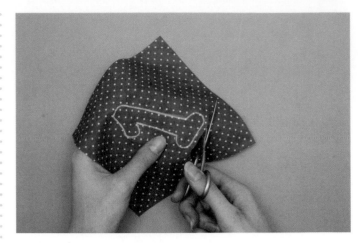

Hand appliqué: add $^3/_{16}$" turn-under allowance.

Trace onto paper backing for fusible appliqué.

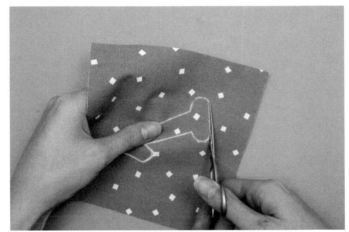

Casual appliqué: cut out on line.

4. For **hand appliqué**, cut out each appliqué piece, adding a $^3/_{16}$" turn-under allowance. Add a scant $^3/_8$" allowance to any part of an appliqué piece that lies under another piece.

For **casual appliqué** and **fusible appliqué,** cut out each appliqué piece on the drawn line. Add a scant $^3/_{16}$" allowance to any part of an appliqué piece that lies under another piece. Do not remove the paper backing from the fusible appliqué pieces until you are ready to position each piece on the block.

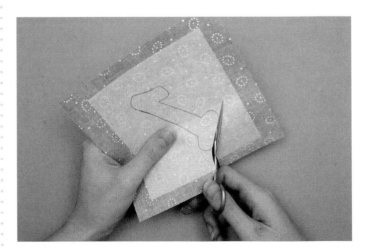

Fusible appliqué: cut out on line.

Making the Positioning Overlay

The positioning overlay is a piece of clear vinyl that is used to position each appliqué piece accurately on the block. The overlay is easy to make and use, and it makes your projects portable. It can be used with just about any appliqué method.

You can find Quilter's Vinyl in quilt shops. It is 18″ wide for easy handling and comes with a tissue paper liner. Keep the tissue paper!

You can also use upholstery vinyl that can be found in fabric shops that carry upholstery fabric, and sometimes even in hardware stores. Buy clear vinyl that doesn't stretch easily and that can be pinned through.

1. Cut a piece of the vinyl, with its tissue-paper lining, to the finished size of each block or border. Set aside the tissue paper until you are ready to fold or store the overlay.

2. Work directly from the patterns in this book or make a copy of them to work from. Tape the pattern pieces together as needed.

3. Tape the pattern onto a table.

4. Tape the vinyl over the pattern. Use a ruler and a Sharpie Permanent Ultra Fine Point Marker to draw the pattern's horizontal and vertical centerlines onto the vinyl.

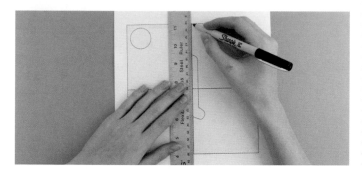

Tape vinyl over pattern and draw centerlines.

5. Accurately trace all the lines from the pattern onto the vinyl. The numbers on the pattern indicate the stitching sequence—include these numbers on the overlay. They also tell you which side of the overlay is the right side.

6. Draw a small X in one corner of the placement overlay.

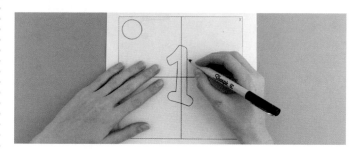

Trace pattern onto vinyl. Draw small X in one corner of overlay.

7. To store the overlay, place the tissue paper over the drawn side of the overlay and fold or roll them together.

Using the Positioning Overlay

1. Place the background right side up on the work surface. For **hand appliqué** and **casual appliqué**, we like to work on top of our sandpaper board. The sandpaper will keep the background from shifting as you position appliqué pieces on the block. However, for **fusible appliqué**, work on your ironing surface.

2. Place the overlay right side up on top of the background.

3. Line up the center grid in your background with the center grid of the overlay. Place the X on the overlay in the same corner as the X on the block.

4. Pin the overlay if necessary to keep it from shifting out of position. Flat, flower-head pins work best.

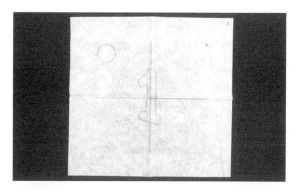

Place overlay on background and line up grids.

5. For **hand appliqué**, finger-press the turn-under allowances before placing the appliqué pieces on the block. This is not necessary for casual or fusible appliqué but is a *very important step* for hand appliqué. As you finger-press, make sure that the drawn line is pressed to the back. This one step makes needle-turning the turn-under allowance much easier.

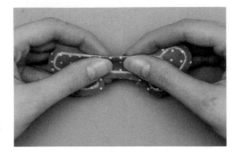

Finger-press each piece with drawn line to back.

FINGER-PRESSING

It bears repeating—finger-pressing is a very important step in needle-turn hand appliqué! You'll be amazed at how much easier this one step makes needle-turning the turn-under allowance.

Hold the appliqué piece right side up. Use your thumb and index finger to turn the turn-under allowance to the back of the appliqué so that the chalk line is just barely turned under. If you can see the chalk line on the top of your appliqué it will be visible after it is sewn.

Use your fingers to press a crease into the fabric along the inside of the chalk line. Good-quality 100% cotton will hold a finger-press very well. Do not wet your fingers or use starch or scrape your fingernail along the crease. Just pinch it with your fingertips. Finger-press every edge that will be sewn down.

6. For **fusible appliqué**, peel off the paper backing from each appliqué piece as you go. Be careful not to stretch or ravel the outer edges.

7. Place the appliqué pieces right side up under the overlay but on top of the background. It is easy to tell when the appliqué pieces are in position under the overlay. Start with the #1 appliqué piece and be sure to place the appliqué pieces in numerical order. Position one piece at a time. For **fusible appliqué**, you may be able to position several pieces at once.

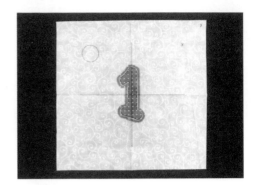

Hand appliqué

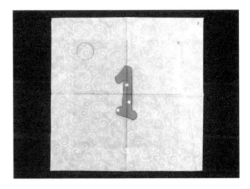

Casual appliqué

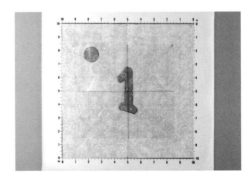

Fusible appliqué

8. For **hand appliqué** and **casual appliqué**, fold the overlay back and pin the appliqué pieces in place. You can pin against the sandpaper board; doing so does not dull the pins. We usually position and stitch only 1 or 2 pieces at a time. Remove the vinyl overlay before stitching.

For **hand appliqué**, use ½″ sequin pins and place pins parallel to the edges. For **casual appliqué**, use long, fine, glass-head pins, placing them perpendicular to the edges. Use as many pins as necessary to hold the edges of the shape in place.

Hand appliqué

Casual appliqué

9. For **hand appliqué**, sew the pieces in place with an invisible stitch and matching thread by hand.

For **casual appliqué**, sew the pieces in place with a free-motion stitch and matching thread on the sewing machine.

For **fusible appliqué**, carefully remove the overlay and iron the appliqué pieces in place. Be sure to follow the manufacturer's instructions for your brand of fusible web. Do not touch the overlay vinyl with the iron because the vinyl will melt. After fusing cotton fabric, we recommend that you stitch around the outside of all the fused pieces either by hand or machine. A blanket stitch in matching thread will lend a more traditional feel on these solid fabrics. As the quilts are used, the stitching keeps the edges secure.

10. When you are ready to put away the overlay, place the saved tissue paper over the drawn side before you fold it. The tissue paper will keep the lines from transferring from one part of the vinyl to another.

Pressing and Trimming the Blocks

After the appliqué is complete, press the blocks on the wrong side. If the ironing surface is hard, place the blocks on a towel so the appliqué will not get flattened. Be careful not to stretch the blocks as you press. Take your time when trimming your blocks to size. Be sure of your measurements before you cut. Remember to measure twice, cut once.

1. Press the blocks on the wrong side.

2. Carefully trim each block to size. Measure from the center out, and always make sure the design is properly aligned before you cut off the excess fabric.

TRIMMING TIPS

- Always look carefully at your block before you trim. We add 1″ to each side of the trimmed size of each block and border. You should be trimming off about ¾″ from each edge of your block. If you are about to trim much more (or less) than that, check your measurements.

- Be sure that your appliqué is not too close to the edge of the block. Remember that there's a ¼″ seam allowance. You don't want your appliqué in the seam!

- Take your time. If it helps you visualize how much you need to trim away, compare your paper pattern to your block.

Finishing the Quilt

1. Assemble the quilt top following the instructions for each project.

2. Construct the back of the quilt, piecing as needed.

3. Place the backing right side down on a firm surface. Tape it down to keep it from moving around while you baste.

4. Place the batting over the backing and *pat* out any wrinkles.

5. Center the quilt top right side up over the batting.

6. Baste the layers together. Yes, we thread baste for both hand and machine quilting.

7. Quilt by machine or by hand.

8. Trim the outer edges. Leave ¼″–⅜″ of backing and batting extending beyond the edge of the quilt top. This extra fabric and batting will fill the binding nicely.

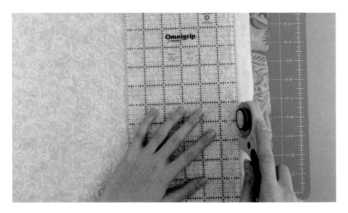

Trim outer edges.

9. Finish the outer edges with continuous bias binding.

Making Continuous Bias Binding

We find this method for making continuous bias to be particularly easy. A surprisingly small amount of fabric makes quite a bit of bias, and there is no waste. We show you how to master those tricky binding corners on the next page.

We normally cut our bindings 2½″ wide.

1. Start with a square of fabric and cut it in half diagonally. Refer to the project instructions for the size of the square.

2. Sew the 2 triangles together, right sides together, as shown. Be sure to sew the edges that are on the straight of grain. If you are using striped fabric, match the stripes. You may need to offset the fabric a little to make the stripes match.

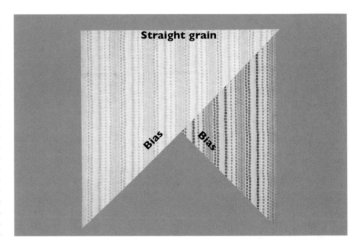

Sew straight-of-grain edges of triangles together.

3. Press the seam allowances open. Make a short cut 2½″ wide (our binding width) into each side.

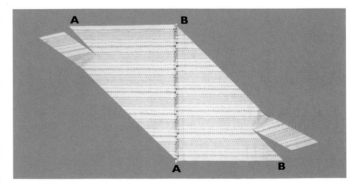

Make short cut 2½″ wide.

4. Match the A's and B's with the fabric, right sides together. Pin and sew. Press the seam open.

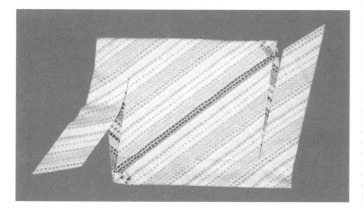

Pin and sew. Press.

5. Use a rotary cutter and ruler to cut through the top layer only. Place the bias tube on the mat, cut a small length, and then rotate the tube to cut more. Cut the continuous bias strip 2½" wide.

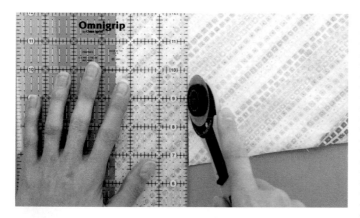

Cut bias tube.

CONTINUOUS BIAS CUTTING TIP

Try putting a small cutting mat on the end of the ironing board. Slide the tube of fabric over the mat and ironing board. Use a ruler and rotary cutter to cut a long strip of continuous bias, rotating the tube of fabric as needed. Cut using gentle pressure—if the ironing board is padded, the cutting surface may give if you press very hard.

Sewing Binding to the Quilt

1. Cut the first end of the binding at a 45° angle. Turn under this end ½" and press.

2. Press the continuous binding strip in half lengthwise, wrong sides together.

3. With raw edges even, pin the binding to the edge of the quilt, beginning a few inches away from a corner. Start sewing 6" from the beginning of the binding strip, using a ¼" seam allowance.

4. Stop ¼" away from the corner and backstitch several stitches.

Stop ¼" away from corner. Backstitch.

5. Fold the binding straight up as shown. Note the 45° angle.

Fold binding up.

6. Fold the binding straight down and begin sewing the next side of the quilt.

Fold binding down and begin sewing.

7. Sew the binding to all sides of the quilt, following the process in Steps 4–6. Stop a few inches before you reach the beginning of the binding, but don't trim the excess binding yet.

8. Overlap the ends of the binding and cut the second end at a 90° angle. *Be sure to cut the binding long enough so the cut end will be covered completely by the angled, turned-under end.*

9. Slip the 90° end into the angled end.

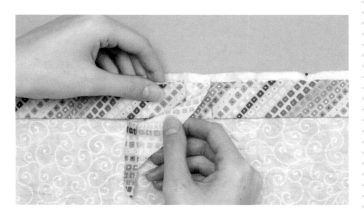

Slip 90° end into angled end.

10. Pin the joined ends to the quilt and finish sewing the binding to the quilt.

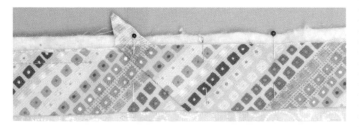

Pin and finish sewing.

11. Turn the binding to the back of the quilt, covering the raw edges. If there is too much batting, trim some, but leave your binding nicely filled. Hand stitch the folded edge of the binding to the back of the quilt.

Making a Label and Sleeve

1. Make a hanging sleeve and attach it to the back of the quilt.

2. Make a label and sew it to the back of the quilt. Include information you want people to know about the quilt. Your name and address, the date, the fiber content of the quilt and batting, the special person or occasion the quilt was made for—these are all things that can go on the label.

The quilt you make for a child will be treasured by that child. You may not consider your quilt to be heirloom quality, but the child who loves it and grows up with it *will* consider it to be an heirloom.

Signing Your Quilt

We have come to the conclusion that it's a good idea to put your name on the front of your quilt as well putting a label on the back. There are a variety of ways to do this.

You can appliqué your initials and the date on the quilt top. You can add information with embroidery or a permanent pen. Or you can quilt your name and the date into your quilt with matching or contrasting thread. It doesn't matter how you do it, but be sure to do it!

We are most known for our hand appliqué. We love hand appliqué! But there are projects that, for one reason or another, don't require hand stitching.

Children won't treat a quilt gently. Their quilts are going to have to be washed often, and might even have to be treated with a stain stick on occasion! We think this fast, casual appliqué technique works particularly well for children's quilts.

Casual appliqué could also be called "free-motion" appliqué. This is a raw-edge appliqué technique; the edges are not turned under. First you sew around the inside edge of each appliqué piece with a free-motion stitch. You can add a blanket stitch or free-motion zigzag stitch to cover the raw edges—or not!

Many quilters turn to fusible web for machine appliqué. The primary reason we do not use fusible web is because it is stiff. It is also true that we don't know what effect the chemicals in the product will have on the fabric over time. We don't use glue either. For the casual appliqué technique we use pins to hold the appliqué shapes in place.

It is very important to prewash your fabric for casual appliqué. Prewashing removes the sizing from the fabric, making the fabric less slippery. The appliqué shapes will stay in place more easily during the stitching because they will grip the background fabric better. In addition, the appliqué shapes will fray less if they have been prewashed.

Refer to pages 48–53 for making and using the templates and the positioning overlay. Refer to pages 12 and 53 for pinning instructions.

1. Thread your machine with a fine cotton thread in a color that matches the appliqué piece. Make sure your needle is sharp. Use the single-hole throat plate in your machine if you have one. Attach your darning foot. Drop your feed dogs. Set your stitch length to 0.

2. Sew the appliqué piece to the block, stitching a scant $1/8''$ away from the raw edge of the appliqué shape. As in hand appliqué, you don't need to sew down edges that are covered by another piece.

In free-motion sewing, the machine doesn't move the fabric—you do. This is a great way to practice free-motion sewing because the appliqué blocks are easier to handle than a larger (and heavier) quilt.

Sew scant $1/8''$ away from raw edge of appliqué with free-motion stitch.

WANDERING STITCHES

It's not easy to keep your stitches *exactly* a scant $1/8''$ from the edge. That's why we recommend that you use a fine thread that matches the appliqué fabric. Your stitches will be less visible. Adding blanket or zigzag stitching over this first line of stitching will help mask any inconsistencies. In addition, these first stitches will tend to blend in with your quilting stitches.

3. Continue in this manner, sewing appliqué pieces to your block in numerical sequence. When the appliqué is complete, press the block on the wrong side. Trim it to the size indicated in the pattern.

4. If you want to reduce fraying, sew a blanket or zigzag stitch around each appliqué piece before setting the quilt together. A blanket stitch will give the raw edges a more finished look. A regular zigzag stitch is a little fuzzier looking than a blanket stitch. Or try a free-motion zigzag stitch for a very casual edge.

To sew a free-motion zigzag, set your machine to a zigzag stitch, change the throat plate if necessary, drop the feed dogs, use the darning foot, and sew over the raw edges. Don't turn the block. As you stitch around the appliqué shape, the look of the zigzag stitch will change. You can make the stitch wider or narrower—this can be a lot of fun! If you use a matching thread your stitching will show less, or use a contrasting thread so your stitching will show more.

Blanket stitch   Free-motion zigzag stitch

Cutaway Appliqué in Casual Appliqué

The cutaway technique makes it much easier to stitch irregular, long, thin, or very small pieces. Cutaway appliqué is especially good to use on the legs, tails, and even the snake in *Animal Parade*.

1. Place the template on top of the selected fabric. Be sure to place the template on the fabric so that most of the edges will be on the diagonal grain of the fabric. Trace around the template.

Place template with as many edges as possible on bias and trace around template.

2. Cut out the appliqué piece, leaving 1″ or more of excess fabric around the traced shape. Leave fabric intact in the V between points, inside deep curves, and so on.

3. Use the vinyl placement overlay to position the appliqué piece on the block.

4. Pin the shape in place using long, fine pins. Place pins perpendicular to the drawn line.

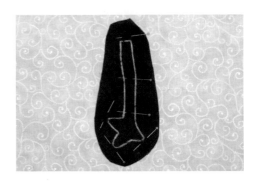

Pin appliqué piece in place.

5. Sew ⅛″ inside the drawn line.

6. Carefully trim away the excess fabric on the drawn line.

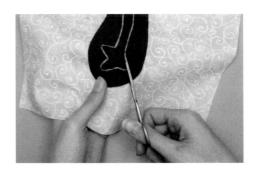

Carefully trim on drawn line.

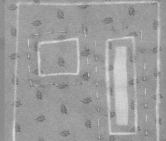

Cutaway Appliqué

The cutaway technique makes it much easier to stitch irregular, long, thin, or very small pieces. Cutaway appliqué is especially good to use on the legs, tails, and even the snake in *Animal Parade*.

1. Place the template on top of the selected fabric. Be sure to place the template on the fabric so that most of the edges will be on the diagonal grain of the fabric. Trace around the template.

Place template with as many edges as possible on bias and trace around template.

2. Cut out the appliqué piece, leaving 1″ or more of excess fabric around the traced shape. Leave fabric intact in the V between points, inside deep curves, and so on.

3. Finger-press, making sure the drawn line is pressed to the back.

4. Use the vinyl placement overlay to position the appliqué piece on the block.

5. Place pins ¼″ away from the finger-pressed edge. Place pins parallel to the edges. Large pieces such as the snake can be basted in place if you prefer. First pin the shape in place, then baste it. When a shape is curved, sew the concave side first if possible.

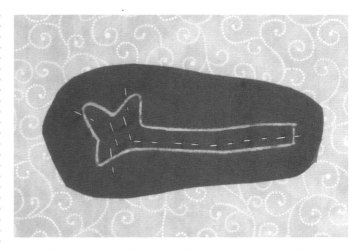

Pin appliqué piece in place. Baste large shapes if you prefer.

6. Begin trimming the excess fabric away from where you will start stitching, leaving a ³/₁₆″ turn-under allowance. Never start stitching at an inner or outer point that will be turned under.

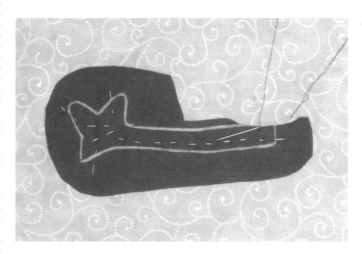

Cut away excess fabric and begin stitching.

7. Trim more fabric as you sew. Clip inner curves and inner points as needed.

8. Remove the pins as you stitch the next side of the piece. Trim excess fabric as necessary.

9. Continue until all sides of the appliqué piece are stitched.

Circle Appliqué

When sewing outer curves and circles, you can control only one stitch at a time. Use the needle or a round wooden toothpick to smooth out any pleats that form. Remember, the more you practice, the better you'll get.

1. Trace the circles onto the selected fabric. Cut out each circle, adding a ³⁄₁₆″ turn-under allowance.

2. Finger-press the turn-under allowance, making sure the drawn line is pressed to the back.

3. Use the vinyl overlay to position the appliqué piece. Pin it in place. Use at least 2 pins to keep the circle from shifting.

4. Begin sewing. Turn under only enough turn-under allowance to take 1 or 2 stitches. If you turn under more, the appliqué will have flat spaces and points.

Turn under only enough for 1 or 2 stitches.

5. Use the tip of the needle or toothpick to reach under the appliqué to spread open any folds and to smooth out any points.

As seen from back: use needle to open folds and to smooth points.

6. To close the circle, turn under the last few stitches all at once. The circle will tend to flatten out.

7. Use the tip of the needle or a wooden toothpick to smooth out the pleats in the turn-under allowance and to pull the flattened part of the circle into a more rounded shape.

Finish stitching circle.

Reverse Appliqué

The windows in the houses and cars in My House are reverse appliquéd. In reverse appliqué you cut through the top fabric to reveal the fabric below. This creates the illusion of depth. The windows are sewn off the block (refer to the next page), and then the body of the house or car is sewn as a unit to the block.

1. Choose the fabrics that make up the windows and the body of the house or car.

2. Make the template for the body of the house or car. Cut out the template windows, making holes in the template.

3. Place the house or car template on the diagonal grain of the house or car fabric. Trace around the outside of the template and trace the windows. Cut out the house or car, leaving 2″ of excess fabric around it.

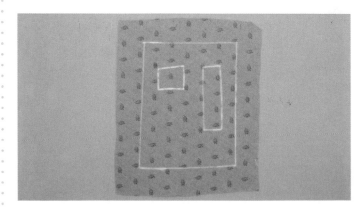

Trace and cut out house.

4. Without cutting, finger-press the edges of the windows on the house or car fabric, turning the chalk line to the back. Place the house or car fabric over a large scrap of window fabric. Don't skimp on the window fabric—if the piece is too small it is much more difficult to sew. Pin the house or car to the window fabric.

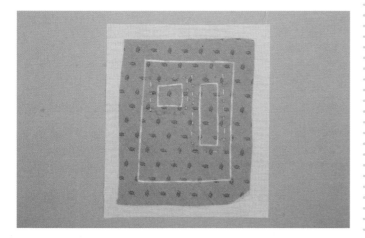

Finger-press, then pin pieces together.

5. Carefully cut the fabric away from the inside of the first window, leaving a $^3/_{16}$″ turn-under allowance. Stitch the window using your regular invisible appliqué stitch. Repeat for any other windows in the house or car.

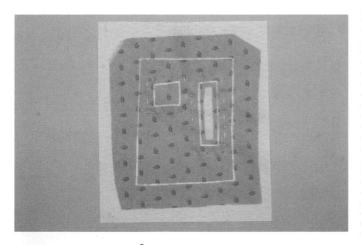

Cut away fabric, leaving $^3/_{16}$″ turn-under allowance.

6. After the windows are stitched turn the house or car over. Trim away the excess fabric from around the windows, leaving a $^3/_{16}$″ seam allowance.

Stitching Off the Block

When an appliqué piece lies on top of another appliqué piece, it is often easier to sew them together and then stitch them as a unit to the block. The doors are appliquéd on top of the houses in My House. It is easier to stitch them off the block before sewing the house to the block. First reverse appliqué the windows, then sew on the door. (You may find that this off-the-block technique works well for the headlights on the car as well.)

1. If you reverse appliqué the windows as described above, the house will still have extra fabric around it. Leave it there.

2. Trace around the door template onto the door fabric. Cut out the door with a $^3/_{16}$″ turn-under allowance. Finger-press the turn-under allowance under so that the chalk line doesn't show.

3. Use the positioning overlay to place the door on the house. Pin it in place.

Finger-press and then pin door to house.

4. Appliqué the door to the house. Turn the house over and trim away the excess house fabric from behind the door, leaving a $^3/_{16}$″ seam allowance.

5. Trim away the excess fabric from around the house, leaving a $^3/_{16}$″ turn-under allowance. Finger-press it and appliqué it to the block.

The Green Country Quilters Guild in Tulsa, Oklahoma, can be credited with bringing Linda Jenkins and Becky Goldsmith together. Their friendship developed while they worked together on many guild projects and through a shared love for appliqué. This partnership led to the birth of Piece O' Cake Designs in 1994 and survived Linda's move to Pagosa Springs, Colorado, and then back to Tulsa in 2001, while Becky headed for Sherman, Texas.

Linda owned and managed a beauty salon before she started quilting. Over the years she developed a fine eye for color as a hair colorist and makeup artist. Becky's degree in interior design and many art classes provided a perfect background for quilting. Linda and Becky have shown many quilts and have won numerous awards. Together they make a dynamic quilting duo and love to teach other quilters the joys of appliqué.

In the fall of 2002 Becky and Linda joined the C&T Publishing family, where they continue to produce wonderful books and patterns.

Bring these two experts home for private lessons!

$19.95, DVD,
2 hours 30 minutes

Look for more Piece O' Cake books from C&T Publishing

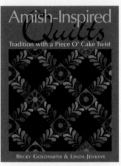

For more information about individual Piece O' Cake patterns, contact C&T Publishing.

RESOURCES & INDEX

Piece O' Cake Designs

Books, patterns, notions (including self-adhesive laminate), and lots more Piece O' Cake information. www.pieceocake.com

Blank Board Books

Look for them at your local craft store or order them online from C&T Publishing.

Quilter's Vinyl

Look for it at your local quilt shop or order it online from C&T Publishing.

For More Information

Ask for a free catalog:

C&T Publishing, Inc.
P.O. Box 1456
Lafayette, CA 94549

800-284-1114

email: ctinfo@ctpub.com
website: www.ctpub.com

Quilting Supplies

Cotton Patch Mail Order
3404 Hall Lane
Dept. CTB
Lafayette, CA 94549

800-835-4418 or 925-283-7883

email: quiltusa@yahoo.com
website: www.quiltusa.com

Note: *Fabrics used in the quilts shown may not be currently available, as fabric manufacturers keep most fabrics in print for only a short time.*

Useful Information

Projects